How to Help Your Children Succeed in School

How to
Help Your Children Succeed in School

Rosanne Manus, M.A.

Tutor's
Press

Charlotte, North Carolina

Published by

TUTOR'S PRESS
6401 Carmel Road, Suite 101
Charlotte, NC 28226
704-542-6471

The material in Section Three is courtesy of Carole M. O'Neil, MHDL, PT.

ISBN 1-889123-04-8

Publisher's Cataloging in Publication
(Prepared by Quality Books Inc.)

Manus, Rosanne M.
    How to help your children succeed in school / Rosanne
Manus.
    p. cm.
    ISBN: 1-889123-04-8.

1. Education—Parent participation. 2. Study skills. I. Title.

LB1048.5.M362 1996   371.3'028'12
                                QBI96-20478

Other works by Rosanne Manus —

☐ *8 Ways to Easy A's in Math, Science and History*

☐ *8 Ways to Easy A's in English and Foreign Language*

☐ *7 Ways to Easy A's in Literature*

☐ *7 Ways to Easy A's in Writing*

☐ *Guided Outlines for Writing Paragraphs and Essays*

☐ *Guided Outlines for Understanding and Writing About Literature*

☐ *Guided Outlines for Writing Research Reports*

☐ *Student's Daily Planner*

Acknowledgments

Thank you Ann Russell with Target Communications Group, Inc. for your editorial assistance and help with the page design, and Carole O'Neil for your expertise and help in writing Section Three on communication skills.

Rosanne M. Manus

Table of Contents
Abbreviated

Table of Contents

Introduction

Parents, do these thoughts ever run through your head?

— What exactly is my child learning in school?

— If I don't help my son with his book report, he might fail it. But if I keep helping him, he'll get dependent on me.

— Bill's teacher called again about him speaking out in class. Should I punish him or let the school take care of it?

— It's nine o'clock and Beth still hasn't studied for her science test. Should I make her get off the phone or let her take the consequences?

— I've already been to school. I'm too tired to go through this homework business again.

— Every time I help Carolyn with her math homework, she complains that I'm not doing it right.

— John's getting an F?! Why didn't the teacher call me earlier?

— This feels like water dripping on my head.

Do any of these comments sound familiar? If they do, you're not alone. Many parents feel unsure of themselves when confronted with their children's school issues. As with many parenting skills, knowing how to promote your children's education is not an inherited skill; it's learned.

How to Help Your Children Succeed in School shows you, in simple, easy-to-use steps, how to effectively manage your children's education. You'll learn how to —

- ☐ Balance your parent role with your teacher role.
- ☐ Help your children build their self-esteem and communicate with them in supportive and nonjudgmental ways.
- ☐ Teach your children to be responsible for their schoolwork.
- ☐ Teach your children to balance team sports and other extracurricular activities with their school responsibilities.
- ☐ Become an effective homework and study supervisor.
- ☐ Successfully communicate with your children's teachers.
- ☐ Help your children when they get stuck on assignments.
- ☐ Determine if one of your children has a possible learning or attentional problem and what to do about it.

The first step in helping your children be successful students is to understand why the job of educational manager is a tough one. Let's look at the forces that make this a challenging job, both for you and your children.

The Parent-Child Homework Conflict

> Why is the parent-child-homework triangle such an awkward one? Why do many children resist their parents' good advice?

Let's consider the developmental stages of children during their elementary, middle and high school years. Children in the upper elementary grades are often driven by a sense of industry and by a heightened sensitivity to failure. They want to be productive and accomplish tasks on their own as they strive to develop a positive personal identity. They want to show you, Mom and Dad, what they can do, not what they can't do. They seek approval — something all children need lots of.

Adolescents in middle and high school still need your approval as much as they ever did; however, they're also driven by a desire to be independent from you and to be accepted by their peers.

Now let's consider what happens when children experience problems in school. They're usually the first to sense something is wrong, although they can't always define their troubles.

When you learn of the problem, you naturally want to protect your children from this force that threatens their self esteem and teach them to handle the problem. Ready and able, you share with them your years of problem solving experience.

Do your children embrace your wise advice? Do they say, "Gee, thanks Mom and Dad. I'm so lucky to have smart parents like you to help me"?

If you're lucky, they'll tolerate your help. Otherwise, they may act like other normal children. They may whine, complain, cry or act silly. They may do everything imaginable to distract you and themselves from the main issue — that they just reminded themselves they're not as independent and accomplished as they'd hoped to be. They may interpret your assistance as a sign of failure on their part.

If your children act like they don't care about their low grades or other school problems, don't be fooled. Adopting a careless attitude is just another way to distract others from what's really bothering them.

Some children do well in school. They regularly make A's and B's. Are they off the hook? Not at all. Some super achievers can make the grade, but only at a high cost. For a variety of reasons, they study inefficiently and must, therefore, work long hours to compensate. They often feel overwhelmed and may worry about their ability to continue performing well.

Let's complicate the issue even further. School is one of the few places where children can prove themselves as competent human beings. If they can't demonstrate their worthiness in school, they have little opportunity elsewhere to do so. To be successful in life, one must be successful in school. The stakes are high and children know this.

Children sense this pressure to succeed from many sources. They sense it from teachers pressured to rush through the curriculum to prepare students for the state tests. They sense the competition among their peers. And they sense this pressure from their parents who know that school success is crucial.

Our job culture is now so specialized that the ordinary employee must be more skilled than ever before. Performance anxiety is in the air and here to stay. We must, therefore, learn to manage it.

You can't make the conflict inherent in the parent-child-homework triangle go away, so what can you do? A lot. Before you read further about how to promote your children's education, though, take a moment to ponder this philosophical approach to the kids and homework conflict:

◆ This conflict is healthy. You want your children to strive for independence. It's this drive that helps them become successful adults. Growing pains are included.

◆ To get a handle on this conflict, you must accept it. More than just admitting it exists, you must be willing to deal with the endless problems this conflict creates throughout the school year. If you get tired, take a few days off, but not an extended vacation.

◆ You may notice similarities between the way one of your children learns and the way you do. Many learning patterns seem to pass from one generation to the next. You must, however, separate your response style from your child's. No two people are exactly alike and your child's school experiences are uniquely different from what yours were. Observe your child's experiences objectively. You may share solutions to problems that worked for you, but allow your child to experiment with them. Don't lay down your suggestions as law. Be flexible.

◆ A key to successfully promoting your children's education is to learn to manage educational issues. Some problems you can teach your children to solve. Others you teach them to manage. Problems like learning disabilities, attention deficit disorder, or learning styles that are in conflict with teaching styles don't lend themselves to cures. They can be successfully managed, however.

◆ Being a good manager of your children's education is hard work. To do it well — to train your children to become independent and resourceful learners — you must put aside your own needs often. There will be times when your sacrifices seem endless. However, when you do the job well, you'll have a positive and lasting effect on your children's future success. And by giving them quality attention, children will learn from your example that a good education is worth the sacrifices.

Part of being a good educational manager is understanding the basic skills your children must develop to be successful in school. The next section tells you what they are.

→

The Basic Skills Your Children Must Develop

To do well in school, children must develop basic language, reading, writing and math skills. They'll spend much of their time from pre-school through third grade learning these basic skills. These skills are the tools children use to engage in higher level learning.

For instance, before students comprehend what they read, they must first learn to read fluently. Before they write long, detailed essays, they must learn to spell, capitalize and punctuate. Before they solve math word problems, they must learn their basic math facts and computations.

Let's take a closer look at the skills your children must build as they progress through school. →

Pre-School and Early Elementary Years

Language

All learning is based on language. Words are the tools we use to think with. Children begin learning verbal and nonverbal communication skills from the moment they're born. To develop a strong foundation in language, they must:

- Learn to group or classify people, places, objects and ideas according to similar characteristics (e.g. a table is a piece of furniture, an apple is a kind of fruit)
- Understand concepts such as color, size, shape, order (first, second, next, last, etc.) and prepositions (on, in, below, above, etc.)
- Develop a broad vocabulary base
- Learn to speak in complete sentences
- Learn to describe events, objects and people in a logical order (e.g. Describe their happiest day.)
- Learn to compare events, objects and people using comparative words (e.g. but, yet, best, most, bigger than, softer than...)
- Begin to understand cause and effect relationships (e.g. If I pour this carton of milk into that small cup, the milk will spill over. If I keep my body still, I can draw better.)

You can help your children build language skills at home. Read and discuss good books with them regularly. Take them to the library to check out books and listen to storytellers. Encourage them to develop hobbies which help build problem solving skills and an understanding of cause and effect relationships. Limit the amount of T.V. they watch. Teach them to entertain themselves.

Speak to them in complete sentences and regularly introduce and use new vocabulary words. When they're old enough, ask them to speak in complete sentences. Show them how to greet people and

8

look them directly in the eyes. Model how to listen. Take turns speaking and listening to them and praise them frequently when they listen well and look at you.

Reading

Reading is the act of extracting meaning from the written word. Since reading is based on language, most children with strong language skills learn to read more easily than children with a weak language base.

The early stages of reading instruction are also heavily dependent on perceptual and memory skills. When children learn to sound out words, they must perceive the subtle differences between similar sounds (e.g. "dub-dud," "man-mam," "pill-bill"). They must also discriminate between similar looking words (e.g. how-who, what-want, confront-comfort).

Reading skills can be divided into three general areas. In order of development, they are word recognition, fluency and comprehension.

Children learn to recognize words in several ways. One way is to recognize them phonetically, or by sounding them out. Letters are symbols that represent sounds and children must learn to associate these letters with their sounds. For instance, the letter "b" stands for the sound "buh" and the letters "pr" represent the sound "pur." Children must be able to tell the difference between similar looking letters (e.g. b-d-p, m-m, and v-w).

Another way to recognize words is to learn them by sight. There are some words in the English language children simply have to remember. They can't sound them out. "Who," "where," "thought," "laugh" and "want" are examples of sight words. Learning sight words is important. Most of the words in the early reading books from kindergarten through third grade are sight words.

A third way to recognize words is by their context in the sentence. If a child doesn't immediately recognize a word, she may figure it out by the way it's used. For instance, "The farmer led the cows into the *barn.*" If the student can't sound out barn or doesn't recognize it by sight, she may recognize it by its context — cows are sheltered in barns.

Ideally, students should master most of their basic sight word and phonetic skills by the end of the third grade. Fourth grade books introduce many two to four syllable words where students must break them into syllables, sound out each syllable, either phonetically or by sight, then blend these syllables together again (e.g. con-sti-tu-tion). Breaking words into syllables and sounding them out is called a "word analysis skill."

As students learn to recognize words, they must practice reading them in stories. They must learn to move their eyes steadily, from left to right and from top to bottom. To read fluently, children must eventually learn to recognize or sound out words so quickly and automatically that they're barely aware of the act. Fluency is a prerequisite to comprehension. If children are stuck with the "mechanics" of reading, of sounding out words one at a time, they have little focus left for comprehension. Reading smoothly is also important to reading enjoyment. Children who must labor to read tend not to enjoy it.

Once children learn to read, they can finally work on the purpose for reading — extracting meaning from the printed word, or comprehending. Briefly, comprehension is divided into three levels of ascending order. The first is factual recall. When children read, they must understand and remember the basic who, what, when, where, why and how information, or the facts in the passage.

The second level is basic comprehension. Students must learn to reorganize or paraphrase the facts. They must put them into their own words so they make better sense. If they can summarize what they read, they can control fairly large volumes of information and easily manage the long science and history textbook chapters in middle and high school.

The third level of comprehension is often called critical thinking. It includes applying, analyzing, synthesizing and evaluating the facts for deeper understanding. Apply means to use the information or speculate how it might be used in certain situations. Analyze means to closely examine specific material for a more in-depth study. Synthesize means to reorganize facts in a new way. Evaluate means to look beyond the words and examine the author's purpose, style and perspective.

As you can see, before students can draw conclusions, evaluate or analyze information, they must first identify and remember the facts. Facts are the tools they use to think at higher levels. Many students with reading comprehension problems have difficulty identifying and storing facts. They may be capable of thinking at higher levels, but lack the facts to do so.

Writing

While reading is the means by which students gain meaning from the written word, writing is the means by which they show what they know. Teachers usually don't test or assign work orally, they ask for it in writing. Good language, reading comprehension and writing skills guarantee school success more than anything else.

Writing starts with gripping the pencil comfortably. The tripod grip is prescribed by teachers because it allows the greatest flexibility. The forefinger and thumb hold the pencil while the middle finger supports it in back. Some students feel comfortable gripping it this way and others, despite their best efforts, can't get a comfortable feel for it. They compensate by holding the pencil differently. They may overextend their thumb or use the middle finger to support the forefinger. Whenever they stray from the tripod grip, they lose mobility and dexterity. Writing becomes less fluent and muscles cramp sooner.

11

The second writing skill is learning the motor patterns for printing and writing in cursive. With enough practice, students should develop a "muscle memory" for the way to shape letters and connect them into words. Once these movements are committed to memory, students are free to concentrate on what to write and not on how to write.

The next skill is spelling. Children must learn to spell words both phonetically and by sight. They must sound out words and write the letters representing the sounds (e.g. c-a-t is "cat") and they must remember the way sight words look (e.g. what, who, where).

As students get older, the need for a good visual word memory becomes greater. As soon as they hear or think a word, their minds, ideally, should make an image of it. Spelling is a perceptual skill, not an intellectual one. Students cannot reason their way to a correct word spelling. As they write with more words, they must form rapid mental images so they simply copy what their mind sees — they shouldn't have to think about spelling.

Many students have difficulty learning to spell because their minds don't make clear images of words. These students must sound out words they've seen hundreds of times before. Because there are so many ways to spell the same words phonetically and because many words have irregular spellings, sounding out words is not enough when used alone. However, it's the only strategy some students have. They must, therefore, practice spelling diligently and learn to become good proofreaders. Asking parents, friends or teachers to proofread their rough drafts or using a spell check on a computer are two ways to manage this problem.

Learning to capitalize and punctuate sentences is next. Capital letters and punctuation marks tell the reader how to translate written sentences into ones that are mentally or orally spoken. The reader must know where one sentence ends and the other begins and when to pause. Students usually learn capital and punctuation rules first by seeing examples of how they're used and then by using them in simple sentences. Then they learn to use them in paragraphs. Students must eventually apply these rules automatically when writing paragraphs, essays and reports, so they're free to focus on what to say.

Phrasing ideas and organizing them into the correct format is the final level of written expression. To flourish at this level, students, ideally, should have mastered all the mechanical aspects of writing — forming the letters, spelling, capitalizing and punctuating — so the application of these skills doesn't distract them as they write.

The different formats in which students learn to write all begin with the paragraph. There are eight paragraph types: classification, descriptive, comparative, sequential, cause and effect, narrative, explanation and persuasive. These paragraphs form the basis for most kinds of writing.

Once students learn to write these paragraphs, they learn to use them in various combinations for five-paragraph essays, summaries of newspaper and magazine articles, book reports, research reports and literary essays. Students must learn how to introduce their main topic, break their topic into smaller subtopics, arrange these subtopics in a logical order and develop them, and conclude their ideas in a conclusory paragraph. Finally, they must learn to proofread their work.

Math

The basic tools students must learn for higher level math reasoning are — an understanding of our number system; basic addition, subtraction, multiplication and division facts; an understanding and memory for how to perform such computations as long multiplication or division; and an understanding and memory for how to measure length, distance, volume, area, time and mass. Teachers invest much time and effort helping students master these fundamentals because their success in the higher level math classes depends on this foundation. As students learn to solve algebra word problems, for instance, they must have at their disposal a memory for math facts, formulas and number properties. They can't stop to think about what equals seven times eight. They must recall it quickly so they can smoothly continue with their next step.

You can help your children develop mathematical reasoning by including them in many household activities. Preparing food, rearranging furniture, following a schedule, and assembling a treehouse or grill all expose children to measurement, quantities and doing steps in a logical order. Have your children do these activities with you. Say each step aloud as you do it. Model the step for them and have them do the next one. You don't need to teach them, simply show them and coach.

Such hobbies as building and painting model airplanes and working with Legos, Tinkertoys or other building materials are great activities for building mathematical thinking. Drawing, working with clay, painting, sewing, knitting and cleaning one's room all involve visual-spatial skills, measurements, quantities and a logical order for completing them. These are the skills students need for math.

Upper Elementary, Middle and High School Years

Usually between the third and fourth grade, students switch from learning to read to reading to learn. A greater emphasis is placed on comprehension. The textbook chapters are longer with higher level vocabulary words. There's also a shift from the mechanics of writing — spelling, handwriting, capitalization and punctuation — to written expression — writing paragraphs, book reports and essays. Even math shifts from basic number facts to longer computations, word problems and other applied activities.

As students progress through the upper elementary grades and into middle and high school, their workload increases substantially each year. They have more textbooks, notebooks and handouts to maintain. They also have many different teaching styles and homework and test schedules to adjust to. Schoolwork becomes more complex and involved with each passing year. This catches many students off guard.

Doing homework is no longer enough. Students must learn the study and organizational skills that enable them to understand and remember more information for longer periods of time and complete work efficiently. They must learn organizational skills that prepare them to write what they know in a variety of formats — from simple worksheets, to essay tests, to research reports, to exams.

Students must also learn to manage their time wisely. Study skills are only effective when used regularly. Many students have extracurricular activities that often compete with homework and study time. For students to do both activities effectively, they must learn to juggle a tight schedule. Time management skills can be hard enough for adults to master.

The need for efficient study habits increases with each year. Ideally, students should begin to learn study, organizational and time management skills beginning in the fourth grade so they'll be ready to handle the major increase in their workload by the seventh grade. The skills they learn in the fourth grade are the same they'll use in college. They simply refine these skills for greater efficiency as they progress through the years.

The degree to which you, as parents, promote the use of good study habits at home will have a significant impact on your children's success. Do everything you can to help your children form good work habits. The remaining sections of this book show you how.

3

Make Your Children's Education a Priority

> Success in school leads to success as an adult; therefore, make your children's education a priority. Here are some ways you can do this:

Establish and maintain a daily homework and study time.

This is a must. Train your children to set aside time to do their daily homework and study. This habit ensures school success more than any other.

When children follow a schedule, they learn to discipline themselves. They also learn to focus on their tasks, pace themselves and manage time wisely.

For many families, finding the time to manage a homework and study period is hard. If you're a single working parent or part of a double-career household, you may not get home until six o'clock in the evening. Your spouse may travel during the week, leaving you with all the responsibilities of running a household. You may have several children who need to be chauffeured to after-school activities, one activity beginning at four o'clock and the other beginning at seven.

Then you must put supper on the table. You may wonder when you'll find the time to monitor homework. If you're feeling overwhelmed by your family's tight schedule, you can bet your children feel that way too.

People find time for things they value. If you value your children's education, which you undoubtedly do, you'll find time to train them to manage their school responsibilities.

The first step in establishing a homework routine is to call a family meeting. Discuss with your children the importance of doing well in school. Tell them you want to help them be independent and successful learners. Therefore, you expect them to do all their homework, study each day for quizzes tests and prepare for long-term projects. If they get stuck, you'll help them figure out ways to get unstuck.

Then have your children help you create a written schedule of their extracurricular activities, their homework and study times and the dinner hour. Post this schedule in a highly visible place. Follow this schedule regularly. Don't allow yourself or your children to break the routine too often. Teach them to be consistent by holding yourself and them to the schedule most of the time.

If your family is pulled apart in so many directions that establishing any sort of routine is impossible, then discuss this problem. Tell your children that fulfilling their school responsibilities must come first. This means they may have to postpone certain activities until they develop the habit of following a homework and study routine. Once they learn to complete schoolwork efficiently and can handle another activity, they may add it to their day.

Organized sports is a popular afterschool activity and one that's important to many children and their families. The benefits of playing a sport are many. It helps students stay physically fit, is an effective way to reduce stress, is a great social outlet and coaches are often wonderful role models.

These benefits have costs, though. Organized sports are more competitive and involved than they used to be. When you include travel and tournament time, playing on a junior varsity team often requires a commitment of twelve to fifteen hours a week. Varsity often requires more. That's a lot! Students who commit to these hours often feel tired and overscheduled early in the season.

These drawbacks don't mean your children shouldn't play. Your children, however, should think about whether they can meet these demands before they sign up. School obligations must come first. When they come home tired and sweaty at 6:30 and want to plop on the couch, they can't. They must study after they've eaten supper. They will have little free time before they go to bed, if any.

Children who decide to play organized sports must be willing to sacrifice their free, unscheduled time and agree to tolerate that overscheduled feeling. It's the price they have to pay. If it's too high, they may have to consider stepping out for a season.

It's hard to sacrifice desirable activities to put education first; however, this sacrifice is worthwhile. If your children learn to make education a priority, they'll learn to make time for other valuable goals.

The amount of time your children need for homework and study depends on their grade and school. Usually, though, children from the fourth through sixth grade need between one and one and a half hours, Monday through Thursday, and the same on one weekend day to cover all their subjects. Seventh and eighth graders usually need one and a half to two hours a day, Monday through Thursday and the same on a weekend day. High school students need between two and three hours each school day and the same on a weekend day.

Set up a study area.

Create a study area so sterile that the most entertaining activity is studying. The children's bedrooms are often not good work areas as the children are too comfortable and distracted by their personal belongings. Daydreaming is easy in one's bedroom, but not so entertaining in the dining room.

The dining room table, home office, kitchen table or even a table in the parents' bedroom are often suitable places. If you have several children of different ages whose homework and study times overlap, you may need to establish several study areas in the house.

Each study area should be stocked with the following school supplies:

- ✔ paper, pens, pencils, pencil sharpener
- ✔ stapler, tape, rubber bands, paper clips
- ✔ three-hole punch, scissors
- ✔ erasers, liquid eraser
- ✔ ruler, calculator
- ✔ index cards, card file box
- ✔ dictionary
- ✔ clock with which to budget time

Somewhere in the house, you should also have such reference materials as a thesaurus, almanac, atlas and a set of encyclopedias or an encyclopedia software program. For older children, stock their station with a compass and protractor.

Provide a quiet atmosphere during the homework and study time.

Turn off the T.V. and the telephone ringer. Use this time yourself to do quiet activities such as reading, paperwork or chores. If you wish, you may work in the same room with your children. They often find studying easier when the whole family is in a quiet, reflective mood than if one or more members are having a great time in the next room watching T.V. or talking on the phone.

If you have very young children, tell them you need their help by playing quietly and by themselves. As they begin their quiet playtime, praise them immediately (before they have a chance to be noisy). Tell them how important their help is to you and their siblings. For maintenance, continue to praise them for playing quietly every several minutes.

Be a homework manager.

Supervise the homework and study time to ensure that everyone begins it on time and is sitting where they're supposed to. Your level of interaction will vary depending on what your children need. If your children are currently doing well in school, you may need to do nothing more than remind them their homework and study time will begin in five minutes and be available should they ask for help.

If one of your children is experiencing a learning problem, either temporary or as a result of a long-term learning or attentional disability, you'll need to interact more. This can get tricky. The more you interact, the greater the chances your child will become dependent on you or resist your help. But, if you don't interact, your child has no support system to help him properly deal with the problem. You must, therefore, learn to interact effectively.

The key to heavy interaction is to participate while staying emotionally detached. As you work with your children, pretend

20

they're someone else's children and not your own. Also, tell your children and yourself that you are not a parent at this time; you're their homework supervisor. Most importantly, practice the communication skills outlined in Section Three about how to talk with your children in supportive, firm, yet nonjudgmental ways.

Don't argue with your children.

There will be days when your children begin their homework and study period willingly and days when they try to get out of it. After all, who wants to study? Children invent ingenious ways to avoid studying. They may "accidentally" forget to bring all their books home. They may say they have no homework, or that the teacher doesn't want them to go ahead of the class. They may tell you they just had a math test today and are doing nothing new.

Kids are very clever at getting adults to justify their reasons for making them study. "Why do I have to sit at the dining room table for two hours when I have nothing to study?" "I just got an A on my last two tests. Can't I take a break?" "It's not fair. You don't make Bill study for two straight hours." If your kids can get you to spend some time answering these questions and defending your reasons, that's time they don't have to study.

Also beware of the child who engages you in an intellectually stimulating conversation that's loosely related to his homework or study topic. If he can keep you enthralled with his fascinating observations and perceptive questions that you're just dying to answer, he'll spend less time studying and more time talking. Kids can be so good at getting you off task, fifteen minutes might pass before you realize it.

Whatever your children's avoidance tactics are, don't play into them. You'll lose. When it comes to getting out of studying, children are often better arguers than adults.

If one of your children conveniently forgets her books, tell her you're so sorry. It's going to be awfully boring just sitting at the table for the duration of her study period. If he says he has nothing to do (even though his study plan for each subject is stapled to his assignment book), tell him the same thing.

If he asks you why he has to study when he just made good test grades, tell him that's a logical question and you couldn't possibly argue with him because he's so much better at arguing, you'd just lose. If she continues to bombard you with questions and complaints, tell her you've both already discussed the need for a regular homework and study period and you won't discuss it anymore. Then don't let another word come out of your mouth. Start singing the national anthem if you must — just don't give her more words to play with.

You may recognize your children's feelings by saying you recognize they don't want to study and are angry with you for making them. If you want, commiserate with them about how awful studying is. But don't try to cheer them up, justify your reasons, argue with them, or let them out of it. Your children know why they have to study. Don't keep defending your homework policy. You'll weaken your case if you do.

Know the teachers' homework plans and policies.

To be an effective homework manager, you must know what your children's homework responsibilities are. Find out what each teacher typically gives for homework. Do they give homework every day? Do they expect your child to study regularly? To read ahead? To review notes?

Some teachers write a homework plan or syllabus at the beginning of each unit. You might learn all you need to know from that. If you're not sure what the teachers' plans and policies are, you and your children can ask them to complete a copy of the "Teacher Recommended Homework and Study Plan" in the Appendix. For fast results, also give the teachers a self-addressed, stamped return envelope so they can quickly complete the plan and mail it to you.

Knowing the homework routine doesn't mean you have to remind your children of it every day. This knowledge just prepares you to effectively respond to specific situations.

If you'd like to learn more about how your children should study, the companions to this book outline specific study plans for each subject —

8 Ways to Easy A's in Math, Science and History
8 Ways to Easy A's in English and Foreign Language
7 Ways to Easy A's in Literature
7 Ways to Easy A's in Writing

4

Establish Rules for the Homework and Study Time

➤ During your family meeting, when you first plan the daily homework and study time, make some rules. Listed on the next page are some rules you and your children may decide are important.

→

HOMEWORK AND STUDY RULES

1. I will write both my homework and study plan each day in my student assignment book and I will bring home all necessary school materials.

2. I will not argue with the homework manager when he or she reminds me to begin my homework and study time.

3. I may interrupt my work to stretch, use the bathroom or get a drink up to two times and for no more than five minutes each time.

4. There will be no distractions such as the television, radio or telephone. I will let my friends know when to call.

5. I will work for the entire homework and study period. If I have completed all written assignments and time still remains, I will read ahead and study for upcoming tests.

6. I may ask the homework manager for help when I truly need it.

7. I understand I may ask the homework manager for help only during my scheduled homework and study time. If I choose not to work during this time, I may not ask the manager for help later.

8. Once I have successfully completed my homework and study session, I may...(family decides on freetime activities). I realize if I don't work during this time, I forfeit my freetime activity for the day.

A note on listening to music during homework and study time:

If you ask a dozen people for their opinion on whether listening to music actually helps some students, you'll get a dozen different answers. If you ask your music-loving child if she works better listening to music, she'll probably tell you it's necessary — she simply can't study without it.

Without trying to solve this dilemma here, there's one thing to consider about listening to music while studying. Music provides rhythm, a sense of timing. It provides an entertaining distraction when a student's mind drifts, which can happen often.

Schoolwork requires highly focused thinking for long periods of time. It's hard to do. But it is a learned skill your children can develop with practice. This also holds true for students with attention deficit disorder. They, too, can build their powers of concentration.

The way to strengthen one's focus is to simply do schoolwork using efficient techniques and without background noise. Rather than rely on a musical beat to maintain rhythm, students learn to develop an internal rhythm. By following a structured study and homework plan and by learning to manage their time, they'll eventually develop a sense of timing and the ability to focus without music.

If one of your children is adamant about listening to music as he studies, tell him you're willing to experiment. He may listen to classical music, or office music for two weeks at a low volume. Absolutely no rock and roll — the notes are too dissonant and no lyrics — they're distracting. After your child has practiced good study methods for two weeks with music, he then studies for two weeks without music. After this trial period, have him evaluate his ability to focus without music. Is his concentration improving?

Most children, with your help, can train themselves to focus without music. Some children have a type of attention deficit disorder that causes them to be distracted by their own thoughts. Children who are internally distractible may find that having some white noise in the background helps them regulate their thoughts as they work. White noise can consist of a white noise machine, a fan or low volume office or classical music.

5

Take the Role of Facilitator Rather Than Teacher

> Your children can accept your help more easily when you adopt the somewhat detached role of a facilitator. A facilitator is one who makes school issues easier to handle. A teacher is one who instructs. During instruction, a teacher has most of the power and control. In a facilitator-child interaction, the child has at least equal power. The facilitator guides the child and shows him or her ways to tackle obstacles.

Here are specific ways to be the supportive, yet emotionally disengaged facilitator:

1. Ask your children as they begin their homework sessions if they need your assistance. Let them direct your involvement. If they say no, tell them you'll be in the other room should they need you later.

2. If one of your children is leaning on you too heavily, is not fulfilling her school responsibilities or is having trouble in one of her classes, first help her define the problem as specifically as possible. Then discuss possible solutions with her and her teacher. With the teacher's assistance, help your child write a daily

homework and study plan. (See Appendix for form to copy.) Post this plan at her homework and study station. Send a copy to her teacher. Then suggest that you both ask her teacher for weekly progress reports. Discuss these reports objectively with your child. Praise her good work or help her change the plan if necessary.

3. Refrain from asking your children what their assignments are unless they first ask you to help them get organized. Also don't ask them repeatedly for their test scores.

When you ask your children for an account of their performance too often, they may perceive that you lack faith in their ability to work things out for themselves. You also give them the opportunity to learn avoidance tactics to get you off their backs.

4. If one of your children is daydreaming, scribbling, or simply off task, ignore it. Don't make comments. He'll eventually learn to handle his time, particularly if his only alternative is to just sit there. If he's entertaining himself with a radio or with pleasure reading, tell him these activities are off limits during the homework and study time and take the items away.

5. Teach your children to solve their problems with this classic problem solving strategy. Model the procedures as you work together.

- ✔ Define the problem.
- ✔ Brainstorm possible solutions and choose the best one.
- ✔ Write the steps to the solution.
- ✔ Follow the steps.
- ✔ Determine if the strategy is working. If not, change it.

6. If your child should bring home a poor report card, count to ten, take deep breaths, then say in a calm voice, "Son/Daughter, we need to deal with this problem. I know good grades are important to you and this report card must concern you as much as it does me." Focus on solving the problem and refrain from making judgmental remarks about your child being lazy or falling down on the job. These remarks won't magically raise the grades, make your child want to improve, or make you feel better.

Remember, your child's report card is a record of his academic performance during a given time period. It's not a reflection of your parenting abilities.

6

Communicate Effectively With Your Children's Teachers

> To fully supervise your children's daily homework and study times, you need to know what's happening at school. There are several benefits to regular communication with your children's teachers. You learn what they expect from your children concerning homework and studying. You can enlist the teachers' help when one of your children experiences a problem, and you convey your support of their efforts.

With some teachers, you can communicate with them through your children, through the mail or from the handouts and syllabuses they give your children. With others, you may need to meet briefly with them in person, at least initially. To establish a regular dialogue with teachers, follow these steps when appropriate.

☐ Introduce yourself to your children's teachers during a convenient time. Don't expect to talk with them at length during those initial P.T.A. meetings when they must meet many parents. Make a separate appointment to meet or talk on the telephone. Have with you a written list of topics you want to discuss.

❑ Tell the teacher how you are managing your child's homework and study sessions and ask him for ways to improve it. Take with you a copy of the "Teacher Recommended Homework and Study Plan" in the Appendix.

❑ Before you end this initial meeting, decide the best way to contact each other when it becomes necessary. If both you and your child's teacher are typically hard to track down, consider sending each other notes through your child, the mail, by fax or leaving complete messages on each other's telephone answering machines.

❑ Tell the teacher you appreciate the work he is doing and offer to volunteer for any school activities your schedule allows. Give him your business card or home phone number or both. Ask the teacher to call you when you can assist him.

❑ Write a follow-up letter summarizing the key points you both discussed during your meeting or conference call. Thank him again for taking the time to meet with you.

❑ If your child's teacher calls you to report misbehavior or low grades, first thank the teacher for being concerned enough to call you. (Say something to this effect regardless of the teacher's tone of voice.) Ask the teacher to define the problem specifically. Tell him you want to hold your child responsible and, to do so, you must both examine the causes and solutions. Discuss these solutions with your child and how she will implement them.

❑ Tell the teacher you can't effectively punish your child at home for a transgression committed at school; however, you will support him in giving an appropriate consequence at school.

❑ Once you've both reached an agreement on a school consequence, get the child on a phone extension and have a three-way conversation with the teacher. Tell your child you hope she won't continue misbehaving, but if she does, you will support the teacher's consequence. Tell the teacher you'll call in one week to determine if the situation has been resolved.

❑ Always make your child a part of the communication between you and the teacher so she may learn to take responsibility for her actions. This will also discourage her from trying to play you against the teacher. (Children can be very good at this.)

❑ Try to accept the teacher's instructional and disciplinary methods even if you don't completely agree with them. Every adult has a different style of leadership and your children must adapt to them. In this life, you must pick your battles. Save your energies for the big ones.

❑ If you have strong concerns about the way one of your children's teachers is handling a situation and fear it's detrimental to your child's education or self esteem, call or meet with him immediately. Tell him you know he has a challenging job and you want to support him; however, you must get this current problem resolved. State your problem clearly. Once you've both reached an agreement or understanding, write a follow-up letter summarizing the situation and, again, thanking the teacher for his help.

❑ If you and the teacher cannot come to an agreement, tell him you'd like a third party to help resolve the problem. This person may be the principal, assistant principal, guidance counselor or possibly the school psychologist, whoever is appropriate for the situation. Do not pose this as a threat, but simply as a way for both of you to get past your roadblock. When you initially talk to this third party, briefly summarize your problem and say that you and your child's teacher have reached an impasse and would like his or her help in solving the problem. Be calm, objective and direct.

7

Show (don't just tell) Your Children How to Do Specific Skills

As you teach your child to learn independent study habits, you'll sometimes have the dubious honor of teaching specific skills. These skills may include how to organize a science project or solve a math computation. If you know how to do the work, then help your child. If you don't, tell your child you're not the best person to help him. Instead, discuss ways to get extra help from the teacher or a tutor.

When you teach a skill, use this sequence:

1.   Model the skill several times, saying each step.

2.   Ask your child to recite each step in a complete sentence until he can say it easily. If he forgets a step, say it, then ask him to repeat it.

3.   Tell your child to direct you through each step as you do another problem.

4.   Ask your child, again, to tell you the steps in complete sentences.

5. Tell your child to do several exercises, saying each step.

6. Tell your child to work independently. Watch him do at least two exercises correctly, then leave the room. Offer to check his work when finished.

A father teaches his daughter long division:

1. *Model the skill several times, saying each step.*

    Dad: I will do the first several problems of your long division homework. Listen carefully as I go through the steps. The problem is two hundred, ninety-six divided by four. The four steps I must remember to use when dividing are — divide, multiply, subtract and bring down. That's divide, multiply, subtract, bring down.

    My first step in this problem is to divide. Four won't go into two, so I divide four into twenty-nine. Four goes into twenty-nine seven times. I write the number seven above the nine in the number twenty-nine. Next I multiply four times seven. Four times seven is twenty-eight. I write it under the twenty-nine. The third step is to subtract. Twenty-nine subtract twenty-eight is one. The last step is to bring down. I bring down the next number, six, and write it beside the number one.

    Now I start all over again with divide, multiply, subtract, bring down. I divide four into sixteen... ...Watch me carefully as I do another problem. Be sure to listen to each step I use. The next problem is ...

2. *Ask your child to recite each step in a complete sentence until she can say it easily. If she forgets a step, say it, then ask her to repeat it.*

Dad: Listen carefully again to the steps I use. First I divide, second I multiply, third I subtract, and fourth I bring down. Tell me the four steps to long division.

Kit: Divide, multiply, bring down.

Dad: The four steps to long division are divide, multiply, *subtract* and bring down. Say them with me. The four steps to long division are ... (child recites steps with parent).

Dad: You said them well that time. Say the steps again in a full sentence. "The four steps..."

Kit: The four steps to long division are...

3. *Tell your child to direct you through each step as you do another problem.*

Dad: You're catching on fast. Direct me as I do this next problem. What do I do first? Tell me in complete sentences.

Kit: First you divide the number five into twelve. It goes in two times.

Dad: Very good. Where do I write the number two?

Kit: You write it above the twelve.

Dad: I write it above the two in the number twelve. Where do I write the number two?

Kit: Above the two.

Dad: Speak in a full sentence, please. I write the number two above ...

Kit: Dad, this is so dumb. You write the number two above the two in twelve.

Dad: That's right. What do I do next?...

4. *Ask your child, again, to tell you the steps in complete sentences.*

Dad: You directed me very well. Let's review the steps once more. In a full sentence, what are the four steps to long division?

Kit: The four steps in a long division problem are...

5. *Tell your child to do several problems, saying each step.*

Dad: Good sentences, Kit. Do the next several problems, saying each step aloud. I'll assist when necessary.

Kit: (With verbal assistance from Dad) First I divide the eight into thirty-four. It goes in four times. I write the four above the four in the number thirty-four. Next, I multiply...

6. *Tell your child to work independently. Watch her do at least two exercises correctly, then leave the room. Offer to check her work when finished.*

Dad: You did those problems very well. You wrote your numbers neatly and on the lines. I'll watch you do two more problems. If you do those well, I'll leave you alone and check on you later.

A mother models the steps for proofreading a report:

1. *Model the skill several times, saying each step.*

Mom: Sam, I'm going to proofread the first two sentences of your report. Notice how slowly I read and how I concentrate on capitals, punctuation and spelling. Those three areas again are capitals, punctuation and spelling.

"The grizzly bears once very numerous are now an indangered species." You capitalized the beginning of the sentence and put a period at the end. Good. "Once very numerous" is an insert so I will put commas before and after it. "Endangered" is spelled with an "e" instead of an "i" so I will correct that. The rest of the words are correctly spelled.

The next sentence says, "There are several reasons..." You capitalized, spelled and punctuated it correctly. Very good.

2. *Ask your child to recite each step in a complete sentence until he can say it easily. If he forgets a step, say it, then ask him to repeat it.*

Mom: Sam, before I read the next sentence, tell me how fast I should read.

Sam: You should read slowly, like a baby.

Mom: Good idea. What will I look for?

Sam: You'll look for mistakes.

38

Mom: What kinds of mistakes? State the three types.

Sam: You'll look for misspelled words and words that should be capitalized. I can't remember the other.

Mom: I'll also check for correct punctuation. What's the last thing I'll check for?

Sam: Punctuation... I know, I know, full sentence. You'll check the punctuation.

Mom: Good sentence. Let's review what to look for. The three things to check are capitals, punctuation and spelling. What three things will you check?

Sam: I'll check capitals, punctuation and spelling.

Mom: Excellent answer!

3. *Tell your child to direct you through each step as you do another problem.*

Mom: As I read the next sentence, tell me what to look for. "Cutting down forests and developing the land are two of the biggest threats to the grizzly bears." What do I look for first?

Sam: Check for capitals. Everything is correct.

Mom: Good. What do I check next? ...

4. *Ask your child, again, to tell you the steps in complete sentences.*

Mom: You directed me well. What three things will you look for as you proofread the next one? Remember to tell me in a full sentence.

Sam: Here we go again. I'll look for...

Mom: You have a great memory! And thank you for working so pleasantly with me.

5. **Tell your child to do several problems, saying each step.**

Mom: Read the next sentence aloud and slowly. I'll help you with the spelling if you need it.

Sam: "The third danger to the grizzly bear is..."

Mom: Read very slowly, "The third danger..." (Mother models the correct speed.)

Sam: I don't know why you make me read so slowly. I can find mistakes reading fast.

Mom: (Listens to Sam but does not directly respond. Then she repeats the direction in a neutral tone.) Begin reading, "The third danger..."

Sam: "The third danger..."

6. **Tell your child to work independently. Watch him do at least two more sentences correctly, then leave the room. Offer to check his work when finished.**

Mom: You proofread those last few sentences at a steady speed. Now do two more. (Mother watches child and monitors his pace and accuracy.) Now I'll leave you to the rest. When you've proofread the entire report three times, I'll check it a final time. Catch as many mistakes as you can before you give the report back to me.

8

Communicate with Your Children in Supportive and Nonjudgmental Ways

Because children are sensitive creatures who need regular reminders of their self-worth, how we parents and teachers communicate with them strongly impacts their development. Most of us want to do everything we can to help children develop self-confidence and a good feeling about themselves. The question is, do we consistently communicate this desire to our children? Or do we sometimes get swept away by our frustration and anger and convey messages we really don't want to send?

What is good communication anyway and why don't children listen to us when we try to help them? How can we teachers and parents improve our communication skills so conversations with our children are supportive, warm and open? This section explores the answers to these questions.

What Good Communication Is

Communication is the process of sending verbal and non-verbal messages that express our thoughts, feelings and wishes. Good communication is simply this — the message sent is the message received.

As the speaker, you want your child to perceive your message in the way you intended. Of the two components, the message sent and the message received, the one that's received is the most important because that is what's acted on. For messages to be clearly relayed, both the speaker and listener must open their personal boundaries and let the other in.

The Barriers to Good Communication

Several factors can prevent you and your children from communicating effectively. These factors are usually emotional ones. When you speak to your children about a school problem, you and they may also convey emotions that impair effective communication.

Let's say your child's teacher calls you to report that your child has not turned in four homework assignments. If you're feeling anxious or angry about this when you speak with your child, and he's feeling guilty to begin with, your words may put him in a defensive state. Defensive people don't listen.

Your words may sound neutral to you, "Why didn't you turn in your homework?" Because your child is feeling defensive, however, and because your body posture and tone of voice may convey something different, he may perceive hidden statements in your message, like, "I'm disappointed in you," or "You let me down." These hidden messages are what your child will react to. His defensiveness and your anger impair your abilities to communicate and handle the problem as a team.

Besides our emotional state, there are other barriers to effective communication. Barriers for the speaker are:

◆ Evaluating, judging or blaming the listener

This threatens the listener and puts her on the defensive. Examples are:

— "How can you be so forgetful?"
— "I wish you'd take more pride in the way you look. Then maybe you wouldn't dress in those rags."
— "Why don't you try to be more like your sister?"

◆ Controlling the conversation and the solutions to the problem

This includes trying to change your child's attitude, influence his behavior or give advice. Your child may perceive that you feel he's inadequate, since he needs all this help and can't do much without you. Reassuring your child may also turn him off. When you reassure, you may unintentionally give the message that his sad or angry feelings are not acceptable and you want them to change. Therefore, you will try to cheer him up. Examples of controlling statements are:

— "Don't feel so bad. I'm sure your teacher didn't mean it that way."
— "I'm going to call that boy's parents and tell them I won't tolerate his picking on you."

◆ Conveying your superiority and certainty

These kinds of comments may be true and at times appropriate; however, they aren't the most helpful when trying to solve problems. Examples are:

— "I'm your father. Now do as I say."
— "Son, I was your age once. I can help you."
— "I know what I'm talking about."

◆ Asking lots of questions while your child is trying to explain a situation or express a feeling

This may make her feel interrogated and, again, put her on the defensive.

Barriers to effective listening include:

◆ Thinking of how you'll respond rather than listening

◆ Judging the speaker — not listening with an open mind

◆ Faking listening while thinking of one's own concerns and not the speaker's

How to Communicate and Solve Problems Effectively

Recognize that both you and your children may often feel touchy about school problems — they can be sensitive issues. The key to good communication, therefore, is to speak in such a way that reduces defensiveness and encourages openness.

When you address a problem with your child's behavior or school situation, focus on the problem and not on your child's worthiness. An easy way to do this is to use the "I-message."

An "I-message" is a message that expresses your feelings in such a way that you take responsibility for them. You don't dump them on your child. You connect your feeling to a specific situation or behavior and you state the desired outcome.

The formula for the "I-message" is:

I feel —————— when —————— and I want you to —————— .

Examples are:

- "I feel annoyed when I'm interrupted on the phone. I want you to wait until I'm off the phone, then I'll listen to you."

- "I'm angry that I asked you to set the table twice and you still didn't do it. I want you to follow my directions the first time I tell you."

- "I get annoyed when I have to wake you up three times and push you to get ready for school. Starting tomorrow, I will wake you once. I hope you'll get ready by yourself. I know you can do it. If you don't get up and you miss your bus, I won't take you to school. You'll have to (stay home, come to work with me, take a taxi using your money, etc.)"

Use the "I-message" for positive behavior, too. Examples are:

- "I feel good about you getting yourself up and ready for school this morning. You really took responsibility. Keep it up!"

- "I enjoyed working with you today. You concentrated on these definitions and spoke politely to me. Thank you."

Use specific feedback. It often has more impact than general feedback and it tells your child what behavior to repeat. For instance:

- "You're doing these math problems carefully and at a steady speed," may have more effect than, "You're doing well."

More Tips on Sending Effective Messages

♦ Describe the behavior or situation. Don't evaluate your child's character traits.

Do say, "Your teacher says you failed English because you didn't turn in six homework assignments."

Don't say, "What are you trying to do, win the 'Laziest Student of the Year' award?"

♦ Indicate your desire to solve the problem together, rather than take complete control.

Do say, "You and I must deal with this problem of you not doing your homework."

Don't say, "That's it. You're grounded for the next month. No talking on the telephone and no going out with your friends. Your life is over until you pull up your grades."

♦ Define the problem objectively.

Do say, "What's preventing you from turning in your work?"

Don't say, "Why didn't you turn in your homework?"

Refrain from beginning your questions with "why." "Why" has a way of making people feel they're on the witness stand. "What is preventing you from..." reduces your child's defensiveness and encourages her to think about those factors that prevent her from doing her homework.

◆ Express empathy. Reaffirm your child's self-worth as you discuss the problem. This teaches him to separate his self-worth from his behavior.

Do say, "I know that doing well in school is important to you. I'm sure this failing grade bothers you as much as it does me. Let's look at this problem objectively and solve it."

Don't say, "If you like getting F's, fine. You'll also like staying in your room every day after school."

◆ As you discuss a problem, touch your child. Put your arm around him or a hand on his shoulder. Sit closely to him. Touching conveys more warmth and empathy than anything you can say. This, again, reduces the negative emotions you both may have concerning the problem.

◆ Be willing to experiment with the solutions. Children are more likely to cooperate when they have a say than if they've been handed a life sentence.

Do say, "I understand you often forget to write your assignments in your planner. It gets busy and noisy during dismissal time and you may have other things on your mind. What do you think about this experiment? We'll have your teacher initial your assignment book for the next two weeks. One week from this Friday, the three of us will talk and decide if this helped you get in the habit of writing down your homework assignments."

Don't say, "You'll do this my way. I want your teacher to initial your assignment book every day to make sure you're writing your assignments correctly."

Praise Your Children

Praising your children for their efforts to do well is a powerful motivator. It helps your children develop a positive self identity. When you tell your children in various ways you think they're valuable, they learn to value themselves.

Direct feedback helps shape your children's study behavior. During the early stages of the homework/study training program, praise your children for their efforts to do well every few minutes.

Since their study behavior during this early stage will probably leave much to be desired, compliment them on any effort you see, however small. Catch them being good, even if they were good by accident. You have to start somewhere, so start with small behaviors.

As they progress, you may decrease the frequency of your positive feedback, but don't discontinue it entirely. We all like compliments, no matter how old or skilled. Praise each of your children a minimum of five times a day.

Make your comments specific. What exactly did you like about their behavior? Specific praise usually gives your children greater pleasure than general praise.

For example, instead of saying, "Good work," you might make these comments:

"You began your homework session on time. That's very responsible of you."

"You brought home all the books you need to study. Good planning."

"You've been concentrating hard for ten minutes now. Your ability to focus is getting stronger."

Hold Family Meetings Once a Week

Hold family meetings each week where everyone communicates without being distracted. Allow each family member a turn to speak about anything he or she desires. (If a person does not wish to speak, that's okay too.) You all might discuss individual successes or a problem someone is having and possible solutions to it.

Encourage your children to take responsibility for solutions by making open ended and nonjudgmental comments such as these:

"Patty, how do you feel about the new time for your study period? Is it working for you?"

"Greg, you were late for school twice this week. What's preventing you from getting there on time?"

"Children, I get irritated when I come home from work and hear you fighting. My first reaction is to yell at you myself. What can we do about this so we can all have a pleasant evening?"

When you gather the family for weekly meetings, you give your children several messages:

- ✔ Their opinion counts.
- ✔ They are valued and have an important role in the family.
- ✔ The family supports each other.

Weekly meetings help to balance the hectic pace individual family members maintain during the week. At least once a week, you all operate as a unit, not as individual members going separate ways. If you have family dinners on the weekend, you may hold your meetings then.

9

Spend Noninstructional Time With Your Children

As parents, you are responsible for many child-rearing tasks. To name a few, you must teach your children how to groom themselves, take responsibility for household and school chores, get along with others, use good manners and speak with correct grammar.

You may sometimes feel that all you do is get on your children's backs about one thing or another. You might feel guilty. Your children, in turn, may feel like they're always being worked on. They may make such comments as, "You're always telling me what to do"; "No matter what I do, you're not satisfied"; and "I'm sixteen years old, Dad. I can take care of myself." Do these comments sound familiar?

To balance your role as caregiver, coach, teacher and supervisor, consider spending noninstructional time with each of your children. Noninstructional time is time that you and your children spend together that's not goal directed. Its only purpose is for you to share each other's company, for you to express an interest in your children and to appreciate them for who they are. When you spend quality time with your children, you convey to them that they're valued, likeable and fun to be with.

Your children will come to enjoy your company too. They'll experience another side to you that's fun and spontaneous. You're not always a taskmaster; you're sometimes their buddy. When your children feel good about their relationship with you, they're more likely to comply when you supervise their school responsibilities. They'll want to please you.

Follow these guidelines as you spend noninstructional time with your children:

* Set aside a regular time twice weekly with each of your children. Honor this time and don't cancel or postpone it unless an emergency comes up. Engage in a shared activity for twenty or thirty minutes. Allow your child to choose what she wants you both to do. Do not watch T.V. together as this does not encourage verbal interaction. If your child wants to play a board game that involves competition, let her make the rules and go along with whatever she does. The object is not to teach her anything. You'll have plenty of time for that later. The goal is to simply enjoy time spent together.

  Activities with your children in elementary school might include playing with Legos or Tinkertoys, building a model airplane, baking cookies, making mud pies, playing with dolls or other toys, drawing or painting.

  Activities with older children may include having lunch together, talking, tossing the football or going to a baseball game.

* During your time together, let your child control the flow of conversation and the play activity. Don't ask him questions and don't teach anything. Instead, express an interest in what he is doing or saying. Be respectful.

Like a commentator, you simply report what you see and feel.
You might make such comments as these:

— "That's an interesting animal you're shaping with the clay."
— "I like playing quietly with you like this."
— "This is fun."
— "You're using lots of bright colors in your painting."
— "My goodness! What a tall building you've constructed."
— "You made an interesting comment about that baseball player. His mind didn't seem to be on the game."
— "You're hoping Scott will ask you to the dance."

◆ You can also make these observational, nonjudgmental and noninstructional comments during other moments besides your special time together. Squeeze them in whenever you find the opportunity. These comments will help you balance your role as parent, teacher and friend.

More examples are:

— "I can see that you're upset by what your coach said. I understand how his remark could hurt you."
— "It bothers you that your teacher yelled at you for talking in class, but she didn't yell at your other friends for doing the same thing."
— "I know it angers you when I make you honor a regular homework and study time each night."
— "You seem really happy about your win."
— "This has been a great day for you."
— "Your sister seemed happy that you shared your toys with her."

Remember, quality time is noninstructional time. The more quality time you invest in your child, the more likely he or she will cooperate with you when you take a supervisory role.

10

Learning Problems That Can Interfere With School Success

Sometimes students have school problems in spite of their best efforts to do well. Many situational factors can interfere with students' abilities to learn. A death in the family, divorce, extended illness, moving, and a parent losing his or her job are a few situations that can cause enough anxiety to make learning difficult. Given enough support and time to adjust, however, many students get over these hurdles and back on track.

Some students have learning problems that are not temporary, but long-term. These students may have learning disabilities, attention deficit disorder, borderline intelligence, emotional and behavioral problems, or, for other reasons, be caught in a cycle of underachievement.

This section briefly summarizes these long-term learning problems and what you can do if you suspect your child of having one. For more in-depth information about these problems and how you can get your child the help she needs, refer to the suggested readings in the Appendix.

→

Characteristics of Students with Learning Disabilities

While most everyone experiences minor learning problems from time to time, students with learning disabilities experience them much of the time, especially during their school years. Depending on how one defines a learning disability, which can vary from state to state, estimates of the prevalence of learning disorders range from 2 - 10%. About 5% of students in the United States public schools are certified as having a learning disorder.

These are some problems students with learning disabilities experience. Because there's a wide range of variation among this population, no one student may experience all of these difficulties. He or she may experience any combination of them.

— difficulty in learning the basic reading, writing, spelling, math and/or language skills despite average to superior intelligence — problems pronouncing words — difficulty gripping the pencil and writing neatly — difficulty generalizing information and transferring it from one situation to the next — inflexibility and rigidity — problems learning to tell time — problems managing time — trouble finishing homework and following directions — short attention span — confusion with left and right side — clumsiness — impulsivity — distractibility — disorganization — social immaturity — overreactivity — sensitivity — low frustration tolerance

The federal government defines a specific learning disability as:

...a disorder in one or more of the basic psychological processes involved in understanding or in using language, spoken or written, which may manifest itself in an imperfect ability to listen, think, speak, read, write, spell, or to do mathematical calculations. The term includes such conditions as perceptual handicaps, brain injury, minimal brain dysfunction, dyslexia, and developmental aphasia. The term does not include children who have learning problems which are primarily the result of visual, hearing or motor handicaps, of mental retardation, of emotional disturbance or of environmental, cultural, or economic disadvantage.

Part of this means that, in spite of their average to above average intelligence, students with learning disabilities aren't learning at a rate that's suggested by their intellectual potential. There's a significant discrepancy between their potential and their actual achievement. These learning problems aren't due to such factors as a visual or hearing impairment, mental retardation or emotional problems.

For instance, let's say a student has an intelligence quotient, or I.Q., of 100. Since this is in the average range of intelligence, we expect her to handle grade level work fairly well. What if she doesn't, though? What if she's in the fifth grade and reading on a third grade level and spelling on a second grade level? If she doesn't have a visual or hearing impairment, or a severe emotional, psychological or environmental problem, why isn't she performing grade level work? What's the reason for this discrepancy between her ability and her actual achievement?

While no one is completely sure of the exact causes of learning disabilities, we do know that students with learning disabilities have trouble in one or more of these areas — interpreting what they perceive, developing receptive and expressive language, remembering what they learn and paying attention.

Learning disabilities are often called perceptual disabilities. More specifically, a perceptual difficulty is a difficulty in processing what one sees, hears and/or feels. A student with learning disabilities may have good eyesight, acute hearing and good use of his muscles; however, his brain doesn't efficiently process or interpret the information received from his senses.

55

A learning disability can include memory problems. Some people accurately perceive and interpret what they see, hear or feel, but they don't remember it. Determining if a student has a memory or perceptual problem can be challenging. Students who don't accurately perceive and interpret information will obviously have problems remembering it. The information doesn't make sense to begin with.

Some students, however, accurately perceive the information. They might understand most everything their teachers tell them. They can't remember it for long, though. Memory problems are often specific. Some students can't remember well information they see, but they easily remember information they hear.

Learning disabilities range in severity. Some students have mild disabilities where their ability to learn is only slightly impaired. Others have moderate to severe disabilities. These students, without proper treatment and support, can experience significant learning handicaps.

We perceive, interpret and remember information through our five senses — sight, hearing, touch and movement, taste and smell. The three senses that have the greatest impact on school success are sight, hearing and touch and movement. Our sight is our visual sense, hearing is our auditory sense and touch and movement is our kinesthetic sense.

To better understand how learning disabilities can interfere with learning, let's take a closer look at the problems some students have in perceiving, interpreting and/or remembering information from their visual, auditory and kinesthetic modalities.

Visual Processing

These are some ways students can have trouble learning information they see:

1. Visual Sequencing

   Some students have trouble perceiving and/or remembering the correct order in which they see something. For instance, a student learning to spell may write "kicthen" instead of "kitchen." She remembers most of the letters in the word, but not the order of their arrangement. Another student may correctly recall all the countries of northern Africa, but not remember their specific locations, even after repeated practice. Finally, another student may understand the teacher as she demonstrates the sequence for a long division problem, yet not remember this sequence long enough to do one independently.

   Some students may accurately perceive and remember the order of information they see, but at a slower pace than their classmates. They may work well at their own speed, yet make numerous careless errors when they feel rushed.

2. Visual Discrimination

   Some students have problems perceiving the distinguishing features between two words, shapes, or other configurations that look similar. They may have trouble perceiving the differences between such words as "what-want," "three-there" and "on-no." Learning certain letters can present problems for these students. These letters, for example, look very similar — "b-d-p," "m-n," "w-v-y."

2. Visual Tracking

To read fluently, students must learn to move their eyes from left to right and from top to bottom. For many math exercises, they must move their eyes from right to left and also from top to bottom. Some students have difficulty tracking their work. Their eyes may skip around the page or miss an entire line of text. They might read the first two syllables of a word and miss half of the third syllable. They might skip the next step in a math computation because their eyes lose the visual sequence.

3. Visual Detail

Paying attention to such visual details as commas, apostrophes, positive and negative numbers, accent marks and word endings is difficult for some students with visual processing problems. Their eyes don't seem to lock onto these small symbols that are often tucked between other letters, numbers and signs. These students may be able to recite their capital and punctuation rules well, but forget to use them when writing. They might know how to solve an algebra problem, yet inadvertently use a positive sign instead of a negative one.

Students who have difficulty processing visual details often lose points on tests and homework grades for what appear to be careless errors. These students may translate a sentence in a foreign language correctly, but lose five points because they didn't write the accent marks. On their research paper, they might get a B for their content grade and a D for writing mechanics, because they omitted commas, capitals and word endings like "ing," "es" and "ed."

4. Visual Concepts

Some students may process such visual symbols as letters, numbers and punctuation marks well, but have trouble visualizing two and three dimensional objects. For instance, they may understand a geometric theorem about congruent angles, but have difficulty mentally picturing this concept during a test when they're asked to complete a proof.

Students who have trouble picturing objects and angles must often rely solely on their memory of theorems, postulates and rules to get through geometry. While it's entirely possible to pass geometry this way, it requires more work.

Other students may be able to tell you how to get from Point A to Point B, but have difficulty drawing you a map with the roads, landmarks and distances in relative proportion. They can process verbal directions but not visual ones.

5. Visual Memory

Some students have trouble remembering certain types of information they see. They may be able to picture a person's eye color and what they wore a month ago, but cannot picture the looks of words for a spelling test or word spellings when they write paragraphs and essays. This difficulty visualizing words interrupts their thought processes repeatedly because they must stop what they're doing and spell.

Some students cannot picture math facts. With enough practice, most students can mentally picture 7 x 9 = 63. They don't have to think the fact — they simply recall what their mind sees. Whenever they think or hear the fact 7 x 9, they also picture the answer 63. Other students can look at the fact, write it several times, but lose their mental image of it seconds later when they look up. They have a poor short-term memory for visual information.

These students often have trouble copying notes, math problems and vocabulary words from the board. They might look at a math exercise on the board, look down to copy it and completely forget what they just saw. This forces them to look from the board to the paper many times to copy one item. In spite of their efforts, they may still miscopy the information anyway.

Students who can quickly picture letters, words, numbers and signs complete schoolwork easier than students who can't. These students don't have to think about word spellings — they simply copy on paper what their minds instantly see. Some students can hold several number sets in their head, making math computations like long division and multiplication easy.

Auditory Processing

Because we learn a great deal by listening to others, problems processing what we hear can, unfortunately, have far-reaching effects. Many difficulties students experience processing auditory information are similar, in some respects, to difficulties processing visual information. Like visual information, we must sequence, discriminate and remember what we hear.

1. Auditory Sequencing

    Some students cannot remember the order in which they hear information. Following verbal directions is often hard for them. They may also have trouble remembering a phone number that someone just told them, or the steps for completing an assignment or math computation.

2. Auditory Discrimination

    To understand what others are saying, one must perceive the subtle differences among word sounds. Many words sound similar. Some examples are: "tab-tad," "Paul-ball," "are-our," "yellow-yeller" and "pin-pen."

For some students, perceiving these subtle differences is hard. This can make learning phonics difficult. Many students with auditory discrimination problems also mispronounce fairly common words. They simply don't process all the syllables they hear and, as a result, mispronounce them. For instance, "chimney" may come out as "chimley" and "installation" as "instigation."

3. Verbal Concepts

Difficulty in identifying the categories and distinguishing characteristics of abstract ideas, and trouble connecting them during class instruction can severely limit students' understanding of what they hear. Some students tend to think concretely. They understand ideas they can see, hear or feel or ideas that have obvious application to daily life. They may have trouble, though, making sense of abstract ideas. These students may do well on test questions about factual information, but have trouble with those requiring inferential reasoning or critical thinking.

4. Auditory Memory

Some students understand what they hear — they simply can't remember it. Like visual memory, auditory memory can be short-term or long-term. Some students have a poor short-term memory. A short-term memory stores information for a few moments only. For instance, when you hear a phone number, you'd like to remember it long enough to either write it or dial it. When someone calls out a word spelling, you want to retain it long enough to spell it yourself. Students with weak short-term memories find these routine tasks hard.

These students often have trouble with long-term memory because the information didn't get registered to begin with. Other students may have good short-term memories, but have trouble storing information long-term. These students may do well on pop quizzes that measure how well one listens in class that day and do poorly on the same information that's tested two weeks later.

5. Related Language Problems

Auditory processing problems can lead to other language related problems. People who misperceive or forget what they hear often have trouble communicating with parents, teachers, friends and neighbors. They may misinterpret a comment someone made and feel insulted or respond inappropriately. They may have trouble expressing themselves. These students might know the answer to an essay question, but cannot write it in complete, well-phrased and logically organized sentences. These students often say, "I know what I want to say; I just can't say it," or "You know what I mean."

They may have difficulty constructing sentences with proper syntax or word order. Their grammar may be incorrect in spite of teachers' and parents' patient instruction. Their vocabulary might be weak and they may have experienced delayed speech when they were just learning to talk.

Because they miss so much of what they hear, some students with auditory processing problems have a low fund of general knowledge about life. Limited general knowledge and low vocabulary is also frequently observed in poor readers. Because they don't read, they don't get exposure to new information and vocabulary words.

Kinesthetic Processing

The two kinds of kinesthetic processing are gross motor and fine motor. Gross motor movements are large movements, like walking, running or tossing a ball. Fine motor movements are small movements. They include writing, typing, knitting, sketching, stringing beads and performing laser surgery.

Students with gross motor problems have trouble processing body movements through space. Certain movements, even after repeated trials, like skipping, dancing, swinging a bat or even walking may feel awkward and unnatural. These students may frequently bump into objects because they don't have a strong sense of the distance between their body and the objects. They may get lost in the mall, drop the ball at a crucial moment in the game or frequently trip. Students with severe gross motor problems tend to break bones, sprain muscles and bruise and scrape themselves more often than others.

Students with fine motor problems often have trouble learning to write. Gripping the pencil, even after repeated practice, may feel uncomfortable and awkward. Forming the letters and connecting them into words may cause problems. These students don't seem to develop a muscle memory for handwriting movements.

Written assignments often take longer for these students to complete, even when they know all the answers. These students may write slowly and painstakingly and all they get for their efforts is a sloppy looking piece of work. Or they may be able to write neatly, but at the expense of speed. If students cannot write legibly and fluently at the same time, they will have problems, particularly when they must finish class work within a time limit.

Long assignments, like book reports or term papers, can pose so much of a challenge that some students would rather settle for a low grade than experience the irritation and frustration that comes with writing the assignment. A low grade is less punishing.

Some students have trouble copying work from the board. They cannot seem to translate what they see and think into the proper handwriting movements. These students often test poorly on short answer and essay tests, even though they know the answers.

Summary of Learning Disabilities

If you suspect your child has a learning disability, talk first with his teacher about her observations of your child's learning patterns. If your child goes to a public school and you or his teacher feel an evaluation is needed to determine the presence of a learning disability, either of you may request that the school psychologist administer a psychoeducational evaluation. Your child's teacher or the principal can explain the procedures for getting this done. In public schools, this evaluation is usually free of charge.

If your child attends a private school, you will probably need to hire a private psychologist to administer the psychoeducational evaluation. You may also wish to use a private psychologist if your child attends public school. School psychologists often have heavy caseloads and can't test right away. Some parents prefer not to wait. At the time of this writing, a privately administered psychoeducational evaluation can range in cost from $600 to $1200, depending on the depth of testing. Some insurance companies will pay between 50 - 100% of the costs, depending on the policy and deductible amount.

A thorough psychoeducational evaluation will tell you, as specifically as possible, the underlying factors that make learning difficult for your child. Diagnostic classifications frequently used with learning problems are —

- Reading Disorder
- Mathematics Disorder
- Disorder of Written Expression
- Developmental Coordination Disorder
- Expressive Language Disorder
- Mixed Receptive-Expressive Language Disorder

The psychologist administering the evaluation and the school's student services committee will also discuss with you various treatment considerations — their plan for remediating basic reading, writing, math and/or language skills; training in study and organizational skills so your child can successfully function in spite of learning problems; and appropriate classroom modifications.

You and the school staff might also discuss such questions as — Is your child in the best class or school for him? Should he stay in the regular classroom and receive help from the special education teacher for one or two periods a day? Should he stay full-time in the regular class with no resource help, but with his regular teacher modifying instruction? Should he attend a special education class for most of the day? Does he need a private tutor? Finding the right educational environment for your child is a challenging but important issue.

Characteristics of Students With Attentional Problems

Just as most students experience learning problems at one time or another, many of them have trouble focusing on their schoolwork. Parents and teachers of adolescents can attest to the low priority these teenagers often give to their schoolwork. Many of them are simply not interested in academics. Their peers and social activities are far more fascinating.

Students who've recently experienced a traumatic event often have trouble focusing. Divorce, death, a parent unemployed, moving, illness, injury — these events can cause prolonged anxiety, anger and sadness — emotions which can seriously disrupt one's academic functioning.

Our fast-paced, quickly changing American lifestyle is also contributing to a growing number of students who can't seem to sustain their attention long, organize their possessions and manage their time effectively. Such factors as too much time spent watching T.V. and playing computer games, and too little time spent reading, engaging in a hobby or simply creating one's own entertainment contribute to shorter attention spans. Overbooked schedules where every minute is laid out for students, rushing from one activity to the next, less time spent with parents, and less time spent in reflective thought also add to our students' growing attentional problems. Students today don't have as many opportunities to strengthen their attentional skills as students used to have. Many classroom teachers will tell you it's showing.

Still, about 3 - 5% of our school-aged children have what is called attention deficit/hyperactivity disorder. They have a pattern of inattention, distractibility, impulsivity and sometimes hyperactivity that persists over a number of years. Children with ADHD don't exhibit different behaviors than their peers; they exhibit more extreme patterns of the same behaviors.

Children with attention deficit/hyperactivity disorder show symptoms in early childhood, as early as the age of two. Some mothers report their children with ADHD were more active in the womb than their siblings. The term ADHD is used with those children whose symptoms of inattention were chronic and noticeable before the age of seven. ADHD is a pervasive neurobiological disorder, and not one that begins later in adolescence or adulthood. It affects most areas of these children's lives, most notably their ability to function in school.

Let's take a closer look at the four distinguishing characteristics of children with ADHD — inattention, distractibility, hyperactivity and impulsivity.

Inattention

Children's difficulty in paying attention can show itself at school, at home and in recreational activity with their peers. In school, these children often make careless errors, misread directions, leave schoolwork unfinished, and produce sloppy work. Their bookbags, folders and desks are often messy and they frequently seem to be in another world. Because schoolwork requires sustained attention, it is therefore difficult for these children. Not surprisingly, children with attentional problems frequently avoid schoolwork.

At home and with their peers, these children sometimes have trouble following directions, paying attention to rules, and they often drift from one activity to the next, spending only a little time with each.

Getting ready for bed, getting ready for school, setting the table and grooming themselves can also be difficult tasks for these children to manage. Parents of children with ADHD must spend much of their time and energy helping them get through the day.

Distractibility

Children with attentional problems are often highly distracted by noises, objects and people in their environment. The slightest noise in the classroom, for instance, can cause them to look up and get off task. The problem isn't their not paying attention — it's their paying attention to too much. Because of their inability to tune out distracting stimuli, they cannot tune into what's important — their work. And, once their thoughts drift, they have further difficulty refocusing.

Children with strong attentional capabilities also stray off task occasionally and attend to extraneous noises; however, after a moment or two, they get back to work. Distractible children can drift for ten to fifteen minutes at a time and be unaware of how long they're off focus.

Some children are internally distractible. Even in a quiet room, they're distracted by their own thoughts. As they focus on their work, other thoughts compete for attention. These children can't seem to regulate their extraneous thoughts like other children can.

Hyperactivity

Hyperactivity, often seen as excessive movement, is an unusually high level of nongoal-oriented activity. Children with hyperactivity often fidget, squirm, leave their desks, walk around the room, tap their fingers and feet, shake their legs, climb over furniture and fiddle with objects. They often have trouble during quiet group activities like circle time or independent reading time. What distinguishes children with hyperactivity from other energetic children is their movements seem random, unproductive and without purpose.

As these children grow to be adolescents and adults, this hyperactivity may manifest itself as feelings of restlessness and sometimes as a state of general agitation.

Impulsivity

Impulsive children often act or speak before they think. Unfortunately, this frequently results in inappropriate comments or behavior. These children are often immediately sorry they acted or spoke the way they did, but it's too late — the damage is done. Other symptoms of impulsivity include grabbing objects out of other people's hands, speaking out of turn or at inappropriate times, interrupting, touching objects they shouldn't and intruding on other people's activities.

Of all the symptoms of attention deficit/hyperactivity disorder, impulsivity is the one that gets these children into the most trouble. Impulsive children often have difficulty following rules. They usually want to comply and get along with others; they just give expression to every desire and impulsive thought they have.

Children who don't suffer from impulsivity also have similar inappropriate thoughts; they just don't act on them. They have a filtering mechanism in their mind that says this comment or behavior is inappropriate — don't do it.

Children with impulsivity don't have this filter. Their thoughts and desires are instantly translated into action. These children are unaware of the effects of their words and actions until after the damage has occurred. They are often remorseful, but must brace themselves for yet another round of the many negative consequences they receive from others every day.

Summary of Attention Deficit/Hyperactivity Disorder

ADHD is a disorder in a child's ability to perform over an extended period of time due to problems with inattention, distractibility, hyperactivity and impulsivity. ADHD is a disorder in regulating one's thoughts and actions. It's not a skill disorder like a learning disability, although many students with ADHD also have learning disabilities, written expression disorder a common one.

According to the *Diagnostic and Statistical Manual of Mental Disorders,* published by the American Psychiatric Association, there are three types of ADHD:

- Attention Deficit/Hyperactivity Disorder, Combined Type — The child exhibits a significant degree of both inattention and hyperactivity.

- Attention Deficit/Hyperactivity Disorder, Predominantly Inattentive Type — The child displays more symptoms of inattention than he or she does of hyperactivity.

- Attention Deficit/Hyperactivity Disorder, Predominantly Hyperactive-Impulsive Type — The individual shows more signs of hyperactivity and impulsivity and not as many of inattention.

Some diagnosticians use slightly different labels. They may diagnose a person as having attention deficit disorder with hyperactivity or attention deficit disorder without hyperactivity.

If you suspect your child has attention deficit/hyperactivity disorder, it is crucial that you have her thoroughly evaluated by a competent psychologist, neuropsychologist, psychiatrist or developmental pediatrician. Because so many other ailments masquerade as an attention deficit (e.g. anxiety, depression, problems adjusting, learning disabilities), diagnosing ADHD is often difficult. You need someone who's well experienced.

Diagnosing this disorder is also imperative because it can lead to an effective treatment program. ADHD cannot be cured, but it can be successfully managed. With the proper support and treatment, many children with ADHD have learned to be successful students and later successful adults. Without treatment, however, ADHD can have devastating effects on the individual. School failure, behavioral and emotional problems, employment problems and social difficulties are just a few of the problems these children can experience if they don't get treatment.

To be effective, a treatment program for ADHD must be multi-modal. That is, it should include or consider medical treatment, periodic psychoeducational assessments, counseling when needed, behavior management, training in organizational and compensatory strategies, vocational counseling when needed and educational therapy. Educational therapy often involves classroom modifications, individual instruction and coaching to increase the child's ability to perform, course counseling and parent training in how to supervise effective homework and study times.

Characteristics of Students With Borderline Intelligence

Students with borderline intelligence frequently share the same learning problems as students with learning disabilities and/or attention deficit disorder. Their distinguishing characteristic, however, is their intellectual potential is not as high. Students with borderline intelligence typically score between 71 and 84 on a standardized I.Q test where 100 is average. Therefore, when they perform two or more years below grade level, we aren't surprised. We understand why they have trouble performing at grade level.

Their performance on intelligence tests tends to be even. That is, they don't score very high on some skills and very low on others, like many students with learning disabilities do. Their scores on the subtests are usually consistent and in the same range.

Students with borderline intelligence often have trouble learning abstract concepts, like atomic particles, magnetism, democracy, economics and algebra. They tend to think literally and benefit most from hands-on instruction about concrete ideas. These students usually work more slowly than their peers and often feel great pressure and anxiety when expected to keep up.

Because these students are considered to be learning at their potential, they often don't qualify for special services in school. They usually attend regular classrooms where the instruction is tailored to students with average to above average intelligence. These students often have good social skills and can relate well with their classmates. Naturally, they want to keep up with them academically and not stand out. Unfortunately, because they're in a learning situation not suited for them, they often do fall behind and are in danger of failing. This can result in their developing a low self-esteem.

Many students with borderline intelligence have a good aptitude for nonacademic skills — mechanics, food preparation, and child care, to name a few. To help them successfully complete their required courses for high school graduation, like English and math, teachers should modify their instruction by setting reasonable expectations, reducing the number of abstract concepts these students must learn and giving them plenty of real life, hands-on instruction.

Characteristics of Students with Emotional and Behavioral Problems

Students who suffer from emotional and/or behavioral problems may or may not also experience learning disabilities, attention deficit/hyperactivity disorder or borderline intelligence. Their primary problem, though, is a thought or mood disorder, intense anger, anxiety or sadness, difficulty in controlling their behavior, following rules, or interacting appropriately with peers.

Children can experience many kinds of emotional and behavioral problems. These problems range in severity from schizophrenia to oppositional defiant disorder to general anxiety. Anxiety can greatly impair learning. When we're anxious, we have trouble attending, listening, processing language, expressing ourselves, shifting from one thought to the next, and remembering.

Students with emotional and behavioral problems often need a multi-modal treatment program that includes or considers medical treatment, behavior management, classroom modifications or special placement, psychological assessment and counseling.

Characteristics of Capable, Yet Underachieving Students

While the population of students with learning disabilities, attention deficit/hyperactivity disorder or borderline intelligence may range anywhere from 2 - 10%, there are many more students who underachieve, yet for no obvious reason.

These students seem bright, talented, quick to understand and make connections among abstract ideas, and they often add interesting and insightful comments to group discussions. They are the same students, though, who may fail the test covering the material they just discussed. What is the reason for this failure?

Many of the reasons for underachievement have already been discussed in this section; however, in the absence of these learning, attentional and intellectual problems, other factors help to explain underachievement.

Schoolwork tends to be linear and sequential. Students learn one skill after another in a logical order. As they learn each skill, they connect it to the preceding ones. Math computations are good examples of sequential learning. To solve a long division or algebra problem, students must work in a specific order. If they miss one step, the entire problem will be incorrect.

In studying the history of their state, students usually learn the geographic features and location of their state, then they learn about its history, beginning with the first people who roamed the land thousands of years ago to present civilization. There's also a logical order for writing paragraphs, essays, book reports and research reports. Students who follow this order tend to get high grades and students who don't get low grades.

When people converse, brainstorm, create or listen to the teacher introduce a new concept, they think spontaneously. Spontaneous thinking tends to be random, unplanned and with few restrictions. It's a holistic, "shoot from the hip" way of thinking and responding. Spontaneous thinking is useful and necessary in many learning situations.

Students, however, must learn to shift from this kind of thinking to sequential reasoning to complete most types of written assignments. They must focus on details and the logical sequences for completing the assignments. This kind of thinking requires more sustained and focused attention than spontaneous thought. Some students have trouble making this shift — so much so that it interferes with work completion and accuracy.

To complete an assignment efficiently, like a book report or math test, students must learn to look at the assignment as a whole, break it into small, manageable steps, determine the best strategy for completing the steps, allot sufficient time to complete them and, finally, decide if their strategies work. Knowing the skill is not enough. Underachieving students often don't have a skill problem. Like students with attentional problems, they have a performance problem. They can't easily show what they know. This often occurs because of their difficulties reasoning sequentially and managing their time.

Time management is crucial for school success. Students must know exactly when, how and for how long to use study and organizational skills. They must pace themselves. Students who underachieve often work at erratic speeds — too fast, too slow or not at all. Learning information and demonstrating one's skill is difficult under these conditions. Brains process information best at steady, even speeds. Many students know what good study skills are, but, because they have problems reasoning sequentially and managing their time, they don't know exactly how to use them for each course, each day.

Difficulty making cause and effect connections is another common factor for underachievement. Many students continue to use the same homework and study methods even though these methods have repeatedly yielded low grades. They don't seem to realize that their methods are lacking and should be changed.

For example, let's say a student who's been making low test grades is determined to earn a high grade on the next test. He decides to study for three hours the night before the test instead of two. It doesn't occur to him that a better plan would have been to review the unit material for ten minutes each day beginning the day the material was introduced. This would have relieved the pressure from studying too much too late and would have improved his long-term memory of the material.

Let's say another student continues to make low grades on her literary quizzes because she can't find the time in her busy schedule to read the assigned pages. She doesn't make the connection that, if her schedule is too tight during the week to read, she should read ahead on the weekends when she does have the time.

Students who have trouble connecting their behavior with the outcomes often make such comments as, "It doesn't matter how long I study. I still make low grades." "The teacher doesn't like me." "Studying doesn't help. One time I didn't study and made an A on the test. The next time I did and made an F."

Teachers can help all students, particularly those who aren't performing up to their potential, by discussing their learning patterns with them, coaching them in those study and organizational skills most effective for their particular class and teaching style, and showing them exactly how, when and for how long to use these skills each day.

The next section shows, more specifically, how you as a parent or teacher can help students with learning and/or attentional problems.

11

How to Help Your Children Overcome Their Learning Problems

If you have a child who has trouble learning or performing in school, no one needs to tell you this situation can cause tremendous anxiety. Protecting a child against invisible learning problems is not the same as protecting him or her from a shark attack. You can't always see or define school problems — they're often subtle.

Many parents feel helpless in the face of their children's educational problems. They may be unsure exactly what the problem is and, because they're not teachers, not know how to treat it.

When you find yourself sinking into despair, consider this: human babies are born with a multitude of imperfections. They have health problems, physical deformities, emotional difficulties, learning disabilities, attentional disorders, social problems and agitated temperaments. They grow up to be like us — peppered with flaws. Some of these problems you can eliminate. Others you can't.

Most children survive, though, and many will thrive, be successful and experience moments of happiness. Your children, too, can be successful in spite of their educational problems, even those problems like learning disabilities that won't go away.

How can you help? Teach your children to be good problem solvers and problem managers. Show them how to solve those problems they can get rid of and manage those they can't. Show them how to be successful in spite of their learning problems. After all, isn't that what most successful people do? Function well despite their flaws?

When your children have problems, include them in on the problem solving process. Follow these steps with them:

Define the problem.

We've all heard news stories about people with a health or emotional problem who've gone from doctor to doctor with no success until they finally find one who accurately diagnoses it. Define your child's problem as specifically as you can and your chances of solving it will increase substantially.

Ask your child's teacher to tell you what she thinks the problem is, when it most often occurs and what factors aggravate it. For example, let's say your child is doing poorly on weekly spelling tests. Look at several weeks of spelling tests with the teacher and analyze the errors. If you can't meet in person with the teacher, ask her to fax or mail you the tests if you don't have them already. Then make a phone appointment to discuss them.

Determine how the teacher tests spelling skills. Does she call out the words in isolation? Does she dictate sentences with the spelling words in them? Does she ask the students to make up their own sentences and show they know the meaning of the word as well as how to spell it?

Then ask her what type of errors your child is making. Is he misspelling other words in his sentence dictations besides the words on the weekly spelling list? Is he getting counted off for those? Is he getting counted off for messy handwriting? Does he simply not know the spelling words? Once you know exactly what the problem is, you, your child and the teacher can target it.

If your child is doing poorly in social studies, analyze the grades. Does she do well on daily homework and quizzes and poorly on tests? Is it possible that she understands the concepts but doesn't remember them two weeks later on a test?

If your child is not doing well on math tests, what exactly is he getting wrong? Does he use the correct procedures but make careless errors with addition or subtraction facts? Does he not line up the numbers in his long addition problems, causing him to add two numbers that shouldn't be added? Does he miscopy his problems from the board or book? Does he not complete his tests?

If your child's teacher reports that your child doesn't complete work, then, with the teacher, analyze this problem. Does she not finish all her work or just certain assignments? If she routinely finishes some assignments, but not others, what is different about the work she doesn't finish? Does this work involve a lot of writing? Is there a particular time of day when this problem is most noticeable?

Ask your child these questions, too. So she won't feel interrogated, tell her you need her to be a good detective and help you figure out exactly what the problem is. Then you and she can solve it.

Brainstorm solutions to the problem and try one.

Once you've defined the problem as specifically as possible, brainstorm solutions. Ask the teacher for ideas and read the suggestions in this section for more possibilities. Discuss with your

78

child an appropriate solution to try first. Talk about specific behaviors.

For instance, if your child does well on math homework and quizzes but poorly on tests, help her develop a plan where she reviews the material daily. After she's finished with her homework, she spends ten minutes redoing old homework problems from the chapter sections already covered.

Write the solution your child will try and include specific steps. Include time frames for these steps when appropriate.

Determine if the solution worked. Change it if necessary.

Monitor your child as he tries the solution. Coach him if he needs help with the strategy. After he's tried the solution for a week, ask him how it's working. If he says it works, ask how it's helping exactly. Does this solution help him remember the material long enough to test well on it? Does it reduce his careless errors? Help him get homework in on time? Having discussions about why something works helps your child solve similar problems later.

If the solution doesn't work, discuss with your child and his teacher exactly what's not working with it. Does it work to a degree but not enough? Does it make no difference at all? Is the timing off? Did your child use the correct strategy with the wrong material?

Once you've determined the shortfalls, modify the strategy or try a new one. Don't give up. Tell your child there are some problems that don't have obvious solutions. If they did, you would have tried them. With persistence, though, you both will conquer them.

Consider some of the solutions on the next few pages that other students have successfully used.

Strategies to increase organization, attention and listening	Strategies for improving test scores
✔ Have your child sit close to the teacher and the chalkboard and away from noisy areas.	✔ Have your child review unit material in each subject for ten minutes every day, beginning the day the material is introduced.
✔ Ask the teacher to write homework assignments on the board if he or she doesn't already. Ask him or her to initial your child's assignment sheet for completeness. Have the teacher do this for three weeks or until your child develops a habit of writing assignments in a planner.	✔ Ask the teacher to complete a copy of the "Teacher Recommended Homework and Study Plan" in the Appendix. Encourage your child to follow this plan every day.
✔ Ask the teacher to give your child written directions to long assignments with each step clearly explained.	✔ Ask the teacher to give your child a study guide or post on the board the material that will be on the test. Have your child write this information on his or her assignment sheet, then ask the teacher to initial it for accuracy.
✔ Make a copy of the "Teacher Recommended Homework and Study Plan" in the Appendix. Ask the teacher to complete it and review the plan with your child.	✔ Give your child pretests that are similar to the actual test. Show your child how to work at a comfortable speed. Model the pace, then monitor your child's speed as he or she takes the pretest.
✔ Every two weeks, ask the teacher to give you and your child a written progress report. The teacher's feedback will help your child stay focused. (See Appendix for progress report form.)	✔ During these pretests, show your child how to preview them. Also show him or her how to read each test direction twice and slowly and to proofread at a deliberate and steady pace.
✔ Have your child practice the homework and study skills in the companions to this book — 8 Ways to Easy A's in Math, Science and History and 8 Ways to Easy A's in English and Foreign Language.	✔ If your child has a reading or writing disability, ask the teacher to give the test or parts of it orally.
	✔ Ask the teacher to allow your child to retake failed tests and to discuss with your child, beforehand, better ways to prepare for it.

Strategies to get around reading problems	Strategies to get around spelling and writing problems
✔ If your child has trouble sounding out words and gets tired by the third or fourth page, read some or all of the textbook chapter or story to him or her. Discuss what you read to help your child understand the story. Have him or her write notes on the key information. If your child has a writing disabilitiy, he or she can dictate the notes to you.	✔ Ask the teacher to abbreviate long written assignments.
	✔ Ask the teacher to give your child extra time to complete tests when needed.
✔ Check the library or bookstore for tapes of the assigned novel.	✔ Ask the teacher not to mark off for spelling errors your child makes on in-class assignments and tests. If the teacher wants your child to learn how to spell specific words, such as literary terms, get the spelling list in advance and have your child review the words nightly.
✔ Show your child how to look at the reading comprehension questions at the end of the chapter section or story to help him or her focus on the important material while reading.	
✔ To increase his or her understanding of literature, have your child follow the steps in the companion to this book, *7 Ways to Easy A's in Literature*. To learn how to understand science, health and history texts, have him or her follow the appropriate steps in *8 Ways to Easy A's in Math, Science and History*.	✔ Have your child follow the steps for writing paragraphs, five-paragraph essays, article summaries, book reports, research reports and literary essays in the companion to this book, *7 Ways to Easy A's in Writing*.
	✔ After your child has written the outline for the paragraph, essay or report, talk through his or her outline, modeling ways to phrase sentences and connect paragraphs. Then coach your child as he or she reads through the outline twice, verbally composing the paper. (Record your child if you both wish.) Have your child compose the paper more slowly a third time as you write it, using every other line of the paper. Your child then copies your writing.
✔ Have your child read ahead on the weekend when he or she is not so tired. During the week, he or she reads on a lighter scale and reviews the book and class notes.	
	✔ Have your child learn to type, so he or she can eventually use the word processor for written assignments.

Strategies for learning math skills and increasing accuracy

✔ Ask the teacher to show your child how to do the exercise he or she is having problems with and to write the steps in your child's notebook for later reference. Then ask the teacher to watch your child do at least two exercises. Your child should say each step aloud so the teacher can tell if he or she is thinking correctly. If you know the math skill, follow this teaching sequence and show your child how to do it.

✔ Do the first two or three problems of your child's assignment and model a comfortable working speed, one that's not too fast or too slow. Then tell your child to do the problems again and say each step aloud. This forces him or her to work steadily. When your child is in class, tell him or her to quietly whisper each step.

✔ Have your child check all math homework answers with a calculator. Ask the teacher if your child may proofread his or her work in class with a calculator. When your child finds an incorrect answer, he or she must rework the entire problem.

✔ If your child is having trouble learning basic math facts, like subtraction or multiplication tables, or solving word problems, have him or her follow the appropriate steps in *8 Ways to Easy A's in Math, Science and History.*

Appendix

The following forms are for your personal use only. Make as many copies as you need.

TEACHER RECOMMENDED HOMEWORK AND STUDY PLAN

Date _____ Teacher _____

Student _____ Course _____

Homework and Study Strategies
Please check all that apply.

	Complete daily homework		Review notes and study guides daily
	Maintain an organized notebook		Review vocabulary terms daily
	Take daily class notes		Read literature daily
	Participate in class		Maintain a journal or write summaries of daily reading
	Read and write notes on corresponding chapters in the textbook		Do extra practice problems

Grading Procedures
Please check all that apply.

Applies	How Often?	
		Notebook
		Homework
		Classwork
		Chapter/Unit Tests (Please circle type.) Objective Essay Combination
		Written Papers
		Projects
		Weekly Quizzes
		Lab Work
		Other

PROGRESS REPORT

Date _____   Teacher _____

Student _____   Course _____

Always	Sometimes	Never	
			Hands in homework assignments and daily classwork
			Attends class promptly and regularly
			Participates in class discussions and activities
			Behaves courteously and respectfully

Homework Average   _____ %
Quiz Average   _____ %
Test Average   _____ %
Other   _____ %

Comments:

_____

_____

_____

_____

CLASS ACCOMMODATIONS

Student _____

School Year _____

Grade _____

✔ **To increase student's attentional, study and organizational skills**

☐ Have student sit close to you and away from high activity areas.

☐ Present verbal information with visual references.

☐ Teach new concepts in a whole-part-whole sequence. Introduce topics and tell how they're related to each other and to yesterday's topic. Then discuss each topic in detail. Finally, summarize the key points.

☐ Give student/class a guided outline to complete during film or filmstrip presentations. Stop periodically and have them note key material.

☐ Give short, concise directions. Post lengthy directions on board.

☐ Post daily work. Set a regular class time to record the homework.

☐ Arrange for student to tape class instruction.

☐ Have student receive resource help for special assignments and tests.

☐ Train student to use effective study skills specific to your class and teaching style. Give frequent feedback on his or her performance.

☐ Allow student to fidget when fidgeting is not disruptive to class.

✔ **To increase student's reading comprehension**

☐ Before assigning a reading passage, briefly tell the student what the passage is about and introduce the vocabulary in context.

☐ Give student a guided outline to complete while reading.

☐ Highlight key information in handouts before giving them to student.

☐ Allow student to highlight key information in the texts.

☐ Offer tapes of assigned reading material when available.

✔ **To increase student's written expression skills**

☐ Reduce the length of written assignments.

☐ Allow extra time for major assignments and tests.

☐ Do not penalize for spelling errors.

☐ Give student a guided outline for taking notes.

☐ Assign a student scribe to take notes using carbon paper.

☐ Give student a copy of the teacher's notes.

✔ To increase student's math skills

- ☐ Teach new math skills using this sequence:
    - Introduce the skill and tell the purpose for learning it.
    - Model the skill several times, saying each step.
    - Have student recite the steps until he or she can do so easily.
    - Have student direct you through two more exercises.
    - Ask student to recite the steps again in complete sentences.
    - Have student do next several problems as you monitor him or her.
    - Tell student to work independently.
- ☐ Tell student to check work with a calculator before turning it in. Tell him or her to rework missed problems.
- ☐ To increase student's attention to visual detail, train him or her to: 1) preview all worksheets and assigned pages from text; 2) read then paraphrase directions to you; 3) list the steps required to solve the problems; and 4) set an appropriate pace by talking through the first several problems, speaking in complete sentences.

✔ To increase student's test-taking performance

- ☐ Give student a study guide covering key information to be on test.
- ☐ Test student orally when that test or test question requires involved reading or lengthy written answers or both.
- ☐ Give concretely worded, objective tests. Do not ask questions requiring high levels of abstract thinking.
- ☐ Give objective rather than essay tests.
- ☐ Give answer lists for fill-in-the-blank tests and limited choices for multiple choice tests.
- ☐ Reduce test length. Test on limited amounts of material (e.g. three chapter tests instead of one unit test).
- ☐ Allow extended time to complete tests.
- ☐ Allow student to retake failed tests. First coach student in the use of more effective test preparation strategies.

✔ To effectively communicate with parents and tutor

- ☐ Initial student's assignment planner so parents/tutor can monitor the student's use of it.
- ☐ Send parents/tutor weekly or bi-weekly progress reports.
- ☐ Other accommodations

MORE INFORMATION ON LEARNING DISABILITIES AND ATTENTION DEFICIT HYPERACTIVITY DISORDER

You can order most of these books through your local book dealer or purchase them from the Learning Disabilities Association. Its address and phone number are listed under "Parent and Professional Organizations."

General Information

Copeland, E. and Love, V. *Attention Please: A Comprehensive Guide for Successfully Parenting Children with Attention Deficit Disorders and Hyperactivity,* 1-800-526-5952

Copeland, E. "Understanding ADD" and "Treatment Approaches for ADD" (audioprogram — 3 1/2 hours), 1-800-526-5952

Crook, W.G. *Help for the Hyperactive Child — A Good Sense Guide for Parents*

Fowler, M.C. *Maybe You Know My Kid: A Parent's Guide to Identifying, Understanding, and Helping Your Child with Attention-Deficit Hyperactivity Disorder*

Hallowell, E. and Ratey, J. *Driven to Distraction: Recognizing and Coping with Attention Deficit Disorder from Childhood through Adulthood*

Healy, J. *Endangered Minds: Why Our Children Don't Think*

Lab School of Washington. *Issues of Parenting Children with Learning Disabilities* (audiotape), 202-965-6600

Lavoie, R. "How Difficult Can This Be? — A Learning Disabilities Workshop" (F.A.T. City) PBS Video 1-800-344-3337

Levine, M. *Educational Care: A System For Understanding and Helping Children with Learning Problems at Home and in School*

McCarney, S. and Bauer, A.M. *The Parent's Guide to Learning Disabilities: Helping Your LD Child Succeed at Home and at School*

McCarney, S. and Cummins Wunderlich, K. *The Teacher's Resource Guide.* This guide lists classroom modifications for specific learning problems.

Osman, B. *Learning Disabilities: A Family Affair*

Osman, B. *No One to Play With: The Social Side of Learning Disabilities*

Silver, L.B. *The Misunderstood Child*

Silver, L.B. *Dr. Larry Silver's Advice to Parents on ADHD*

Smith, S. *No Easy Answers: The Learning Disabled Child at Home and at School*

Stevens, S. *The Learning Disabled Child: Ways That Parents Can Help*

Weiss, L. *Attention Deficit Disorder in Adults*

Wender, P. *The Hyperactive Child, Adolescent and Adult: ADD Through the Life Span*

For Children and Adolescents

Galvin, M. *Otto Learns About His Medicine* (preschool and early elementary)

Gehret, J. *Eagle Eyes: A Child's Guide to Paying Attention*

Levine, M. *All Kinds of Minds: A Young Student's Book about Learning Abilities and Learning Disorders*

Levine, M. *Keeping a Head in School — A Student's Book About Learning Disabilities and Attention Deficit Disorders*

Moss, D.M. *Shelley, The Hyperactive Turtle* (preschool and early elementary)

Quinn, P. and Stern, J.M. *Putting on the Brakes: Young People's Guide to Understanding Attention Deficit Hyperactivity Disorder*

Parent and Professional Organizations

Children and Adults with Attention Deficit Disorder (CHADD)

> 499 Northwest 70th Avenue
> Plantation, FL. 33317
> 800-233-4050

Learning Disabilities Association

> 4156 Library Road
> Pittsburgh, PA. 15234
> (412) 341-1515